Play School Play Ideas

Play School, the daily BBC television programme, is offered as entertainment for children at home. This book contains hundreds of ideas for entertainment and play—things to make, toys and games, simple experiments, ideas for dressing up, rhymes and jingles. The materials needed are common household objects or inexpensive and easy to obtain. All the ideas have been tried out with small children.

Leaders and teachers in Play Groups and nurseries will find the book invaluable, and mothers will welcome a fund of new ideas.

Play School
Play
Ideas

Ruth Craft

Drawings by Quentin Blake

BBC/KNIGHT BOOKS

© Ruth Craft 1971

Illustrations © British Broadcasting Corporation 1971

First published by the
British Broadcasting Corporation 1971

This edition first published by the
British Broadcasting Corporation/Knight Books 1983

Fourth impression 1984

British Library C.I.P.
Craft, Ruth
  Play School play ideas.
  1. Handicraft—Juvenile literature
  I. Title
  745.5   TT160

  ISBN 0 340 33299 9
      (0 563 20166 5 BBC)

Printed and bound in Great Britain for the British
Broadcasting Corporation, 35 Marylebone High Street,
London W1M 4AA and Hodder and Stoughton
Paperbacks, a division of Hodder and Stoughton Ltd.,
Mill Road, Dunton Green, Sevenoaks, Kent, (Editorial
Office: 47 Bedford Square, London, WC1 3DP) by
Richard Clay (The Chaucer Press) Ltd,
Bungay, Suffolk.

Introduction

Play School is a daily entertainment for children
under five at home. It is shown on BBC-2 five times
a week in the mornings. The programmes are repeated
on BBC-1 in the afternoons. Since 1964 the *Play School*
production team have received hundreds of requests
for more information about the traditional and original
material used in the programme. We have always been
delighted to answer all requests and help where we
could. This book – we hope – will help some more.

Cynthia Felgate

Monday

Useful
Box
Day

Boats can be made from . . .
walnut shells with plasticine to hold a matchstick mast
and a paper sail, or matchsticks, or bottle tops floated
cork side up.

FINGER PLAY
Here is the sea, the wavy sea,
Here is the boat and this is me.
Sea: One wavy hand
Boat: Other hand cupped on sea
Me: Thumb wriggling from the boat
An empty date-box makes a tanker with a matchbox in
the stern and a cork for the funnel. Corks make
lifeboats, too, orange peels don't even need sails.

A sailor went to sea
To see what he could see,
And all that he could see,
Was sea, sea, sea.

Try a submarine – an empty washing-up liquid bottle,
model a bit of plasticine for conning tower. Now –
submerge! Fill up with water, replace cap, watch it sink
in washing-up bowl – and surface again! Release cap
and watch it rise.

Sail the boats in shallow water in a washing-up bowl with a lump of plasticine for island. Use pipecleaner palmtrees with twists of paper for fronds.

Or make it an *unfriendly* island with a stockade of ice-lolly sticks or matchsticks and inhabited by hairy monster crabs made of plasticine with pipecleaner legs.

Or cause a shipwreck by tilting bowl from side to side, wrecking the boats onto the shore.
Or take the boats down the river – a length of silver foil.

Row, row, row the boat,
Gently down the stream,
Merrily, merrily, merrily, merrily,
Life is but a dream.

Build up the banks of the river with a forest of trees made from twigs stuck into plasticine. Make a bridge with a ruler supported on two blocks, and some cranes – pencils or ice-lolly sticks jammed into empty matchboxes. Put some windmills along the banks, two ice-lolly sticks pinned across empty washing-up liquid bottle.

Here comes a **train** – or two!

Engine, engine Number Nine,
Running on the Glasgow line,
If she's polished, how she'll shine!
Engine, engine Number Nine.

Cotton reels strung together with toothpaste tube cap for funnel. Assorted boxes, small ones like matchboxes, threaded together, with one matchbox cover jammed into the first 'carriage' to make engine.

There's a **covered wagon**!
A circle of paper bent into shape within large matchbox. Pencils pushed through sides to make axles,
smaller circles of card for wheels and two more pencils
for shafts.
And a truck!
Use a small, light, square box for body and empty
cheese boxes for wheels. Attach wheels with push-
through paper-clips. Knot string or wool through one
end and the truck will roll along.

Or finish off with a bubble storm. The fastest bubbles
get blown through the ends of cotton reels.

There was an old whale called Molly-o,
She wouldn't say yes and she wouldn't say no,
But oh my goodness, how she would blow,
Blow! Blow! Blow!

Houses and Buildings can be made with boxes and tins. Just painting the boxes and tins can fill in an afternoon, but windows and doors can be cut in tall cereal boxes for blocks of flats . . .

Smaller houses need smaller boxes and sometimes roofs. Make a roof from a square of cardboard bent in two.

This is my house	(Put fingertips together for roof)
This is the door	(Put tips of index fingers together)
The windows are shiny	(Pretend to polish the windows)
And so is the floor	(Pretend to polish the floor)
Outside there's a chimney	(Hold the hands up high for the chimney)
As tall as can be	
With smoke that goes curling up	(Wave one hand slowly over the head)
Come and see.	

Two large shoeboxes on top of each other make a good dolls' house. Use scraps of material for carpets, and almost anything can be furniture.

The people who live in the dolls' house can be pipe-cleaner people; you can make a fat baby by twisting scraps of material round the wire.

A cocoa tin with a stockade of clothes-pegs pinned round the top makes a robbers' fort. Make your robbers out of potatoes with matchstick arms and legs.

Castles can be made from larger boxes. Cut turrets around the top, cut a door, but leave a hinge at the top with some string attached to the outside of the door so it can be lifted quickly. Cut out a cardboard princess with yellow wool hair and string attached to her back. Put princess in amongst potato robbers and rescue her smartly. Bring out Hairy Monster Crabs for further dramatic action.

Toy **cars** are more fun in the right setting. One shoebox makes a garage. Stick a couple of matchbox covers in a base of plasticine for the pumps. Push a pipecleaner through the pump for a hose.

Fly-overs and motorways can be put together with strips of card, blocks, rulers and empty boxes. Traffic lights can be made with ice-lolly sticks based in plasticine with circles of colour.

If you can spare them, a box of lentils in a pie-dish makes a very good building-site. Haricot beans, macaroni or rice can also be used for gravel. Add cotton-reels for concrete-mixers.

I'll take you riding in my car, car,
I'll take you riding in my car, car,
I'll take you riding in my car, car,
I'll take you riding in my car.

The engine it goes brrm, brrm,
The engine it goes brrm, brrm,
Brrm, brrm, chrrka, chrrka, brrm, brrm,
Riding in my car.

The hooter it goes beep, beep!
The hooter it goes beep, beep!
The hooter it goes beep, beep!
Riding in my car.

Sheep Farm You can cover piles of boxes with green fabric for a hill, make trees from cotton-reels and feathers, fields from darker squares of material, and ploughed fields from corrugated cardboard. Make farm buildings from small boxes; sheep by sticking cotton-wool on the top of walnut shells or date stones.

Click go the shears boys, click, click, click,
Wide is his blow and his hands move quick,
The ringer looks around and is beaten by the blow,
And curses the old snagger with the blue-bellied joe.

A giraffe– one small potato for head, jam pencil through head and through an empty cardboard tube onto body, which is a larger potato, ice-lolly sticks for legs and string pinned on for tail.

A hedgehog – one soft ball of plasticine stuck with used matches and drawing-pin eyes, or use a cork stuck with paper clips.

A spider– one small ball of plasticine with eight pipecleaner legs.

Incy wincy spider climbed up the spout,
Down came the rain and washed the spider out,
Out came the sunshine, dried up all the rain,
Incy wincy spider climbed the spout again.

Four Cats

from a ball of wool – five long balls for
body and four legs, round ball for head; fix them
together with knitting-needles, strand of wool for tail.
Tie piece of wool round other end of body to make head
– paper ears, pipecleaners for whiskers.

from potatoes – one small one for head, joined by a
pencil to a larger one for the body, one pipecleaner for
tail, two hair-pins for ears and more pipecleaners for
legs.

from a paper bag – stuff paper bag with old stockings or
more paper, twist corners for ears, draw on face and
make a string tail.

from a tin – use one empty scouring-powder tin, push
four pencils in for legs, use end with holes in it for face,
string tail, string whiskers held with sticky tape.

Diddlety, diddlety, dumpty,
The cat ran up the plum tree,
Half a crown to fetch her down,
Diddlety, diddlety, dumpty.

Three Snakes

from an old stocking – fill with lots more old nylon stockings; glue a red paper tongue on the head end.

from cotton-reels – lots of cotton-reels threaded together.

from an old sock pulled over the hand – it's as good as anything.

Junkopotamus
Large potato body, with pigeon feathers stuck along its back, two pencil legs and two ice-lolly stick legs, a twiggy branch for a tail is stuck in the end. The head is a square box attached with ice-lolly stick, glue on a toothpaste-tube cap for the nose. Complete by adding an egg-box carton hat with a feather stuck in it! Or invent your own creature with its own name.

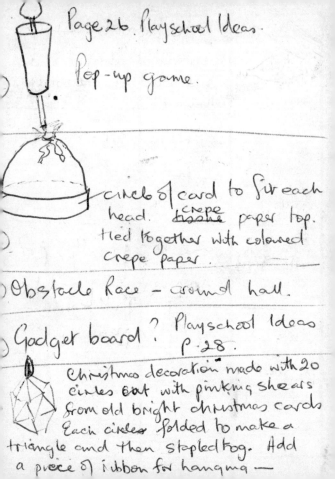

Page 26. Playschool Ideas.

Pop-up game.

circle of card to fit each head. crepe tissue paper top. tied together with coloured crepe paper.

Obstacle Race – around hall.

Gadget board? Playschool Ideas p. 28.

Christmas decoration made with 20 circles cut with pinking shears from old bright christmas cards. Each circles folded to make a triangle and then stapled tog. Add a piece of ribbon for hanging —

⑥ Things for feeding birds !

⑦  Autumn hedgehog shape
cut out and stuck with
brown fallen leaves

Sounds — make shakers?

Baking!

Cut some sheets of wallpaper.
for crayoning + painting
or collage.

When doing <u>Shapes</u> cut
paper out of triangles — circles — etc
to emphasise learning.

The **toys** and dolls will enjoy a cardboard box
television.
Start with a good square box, and cut out a front panel
for the screen. Cut slits each side of the panel. Make
screen from thin grey card. Paste pictures onto it, and
slide these in and out of the panel. Use corks pinned in
the front for knobs.

A Suitcase – two shoeboxes hinged together with tape.

Spectacles – made from pipecleaners.

Give them a show with paper bag *puppets*.
Paper bags with faces drawn on them put over hands
with rubber bands round wrists. Twist corners of bags
for ears. Make a hole in the face of the puppet and push
a finger through for a tongue.

Toys and **games** of many kinds.
Thread a large button on a circle of string and make it whizz.

Hoopla – make a cone out of cardboard and sticky tape, decorate three ping-pong balls, attach them to the rim of the cone with string and sticky tape.

Play Feed the Lion! Hook a good-sized paper carrier-bag onto the back of a chair by one handle, cut off the other one. You can draw a lion's face on the front of the bag if you've got time. Make "meat balls" out of wodges of screwed-up newspaper. Then stand back at a suitable distance and aim for the lion's mouth – the opening in the top of the carrier-bag. See how many meat balls he can eat!

Button in the egg-box Use an empty egg-box and aim from a suitable distance to fill each section with a supply of buttons. A simple version of tiddly-winks can also be played this way if you have the counters. A smaller child's aim can be considerably improved if he throws his button from an egg-cup or empty yoghurt carton.

Skittles Two or three empty washing-up liquid bottles – or as many as you can spare – lined up against a wall make the skittles. You can ward off accidents by placing a cushion or two behind the skittles. A spare potato can take the place of a ball. It will roll well across the floor, and has the advantage that it will not bounce.

Paper windmill – take a square of thin card or thick paper, cut four lines from the corners to the middle, taking care that the cuts don't meet. Bring every other corner to the centre, and stick a drawing-pin through corners and middle and onto end of a pencil or dowelling rod.

Money-box – one empty washing-up liquid bottle – cut a slit wide enough to take the coins. Decorate.

Snowman – unroll length of cotton wool, and wind round cardboard tube. Tie with ribbon to divide head and body. Mark in eyes with felt pen and stick buttons down the front.

A frame for a picture Use an empty cheese box for the round frame and attach some string or wool to each side with sticky tape. Fill in the frame with a drawing or a collage of silver paper, small pieces of paper doilies, scraps of material or cut-outs of coloured pictures from a magazine.

Something for **Baby** – a mobile to look at or to hang on his pram. Milk-bottle tops or pieces of coloured cellophane and card threaded on a string.

Something for Father to put in his workshop – a baton of wood with cup hooks screwed in. Start the holes with a small bradawl and hooks will easily screw in. Offer a piece of sandpaper to smooth off edges.

Something for Mother, Auntie or Grandma – a small, pretty box. One empty matchbox, covered with felt (glue it on), or painted black (wait for it to dry). Then glue on shells, sequins or bits of coloured sticky paper. Or make a shopping-bag. Decorate an ordinary brown-paper carrier-bag with coloured sticky paper, or use pictures from magazines cut out and glued on.

FINGER PLAY

This is our dad, short and stout,
This is our mum with children all about,
This is our brother, tall you see,
This is our sister with doll on her knee,
This is our baby, sure to grow,
And here is our family all in a row.
(Action: Point to each finger in turn,
starting with the thumb)

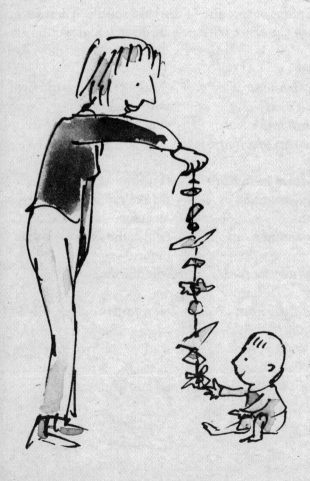

Something for Grandma or Grandad – a string tin.
A golden syrup or similar-sized tin with a hole punched in the lid, ball of string inside, thread end of string through the hole. Replace lid. Decorate with paper or paint.

Or a Book of Flowers.
Use plain white paper which can be folded down the middle to make the spine of the book. Fold them first and then stick a cut-out picture or flower on each page. A seed or plant catalogue is the best source. Then sew the spine of the book with one large stitch of wool.

FINGER PLAY

These are Grandma's spectacles	(Make circles round eyes with fingers)
This is Grandma's hat	(Put hands over head)
This is the way she folds her hands	
And puts them in her lap	(Put hands in lap)
These are Grandad's spectacles	(Make circles round eyes as before)
This is Grandad's hat	(Put hands over head as before)
This is the way he folds his arms	(Fold arms)
And has a little nap	(Doze off)

Everybody likes Sugar Mice.

Ingredients: 1 lb. icing sugar
1 egg white
A few drops of cochineal
Some liquorice strips, peanuts and silver
balls

Whisk egg white lightly, mix with sieved icing sugar and a few drops of water and cochineal. The mixture should be firm enough to mould with the hands. Use the peanuts for ears, silver balls for eyes and liquorice strips for tails. Make on individual paper plates and when set, scoop off with a fish slice.

A **Nativity scene** will need a permanent site – or at least semi-permanent!

You can make all the characters in the scene (with the exception of Baby Jesus) from the same materials. Each figure needs an empty cardboard tube for the body and a wodge of newspaper rolled into a ball for the head. Use sticky tape to secure the head to the body and to make the ball nice and round. Then pin suitable pieces of material over the heads and around the body. Add cardboard crowns to the Kings and some tinsel and glitter to their robes. Mary has a blue robe. Baby Jesus can be a pipecleaner baby. To do this roll small strips of soft material around a small pipecleaner figure. He can sleep in a matchbox manger filled with wood-shavings. The animals in the scene can be potato animals. Small potatoes fixed together with matchsticks and using ice-lolly sticks for legs. Or something more ambitious can be attempted with papier-mâché, modelling dough or plasticine.

Recipe for modelling dough
1 cup of salt
1½ cups of flour
½ cup of water
2 tablespoons of cooking oil
Food colouring if required
This dough will keep if it's put in a plastic bag or a covered jar and put in a refrigerator. It can also be used for making things that "have to be kept" because it will dry out and harden.

Some things to keep. A big monster can be made with a chicken wire base which is then spread liberally with plaster of paris and smoothed off. When dry it can be painted and decorated. To make ridges and curls in the shape of the body and legs, twist old stockings or pieces of fabric through and around the wire. This is an everlasting creation, and can be a useful addition to domestic theatrical productions.

Papier-mâché is a two-day operation! First tear up newspaper into very small pieces – the finer the pieces the smoother the papier-mâché will be. The paper is then soaked in water overnight – use more water if the paper soaks it all up. Next day, wring all the excess water out of the paper and rub into a fine pulp. To one cup of squeezed pulp add one cup of flour and one-third of a cup of salt. Squeeze it all together until it is well-mixed. Now it can be used, but if it is to be kept add a few drops of oil of cloves. It will then keep for a few days without smelling.

Beads are simple to make. Roll the papier-mâché around ping-pong balls for big, round beads, or around metal knitting-needles for smaller ones. Papier-mâché is a good cheap modelling material, and animals, fruit, houses or anything which takes the fancy can be made. Puppets' heads are one idea – these can be mounted on cardboard tubes.

When the papier-mâché has dried it will make an easy surface to paint and decorate – even if it does turn out a bit lumpy!

Bread flowers need a good chunk of bread fresh from the baker – not the sliced variety. Cut off the crusts and mould and pound the bread until it is soft and pliable again. Take small pieces and roll into a tiny ball between the thumb and finger. Then press out flat and as thin as possible and shape into petal forms. These can be squeezed together at the base to make a small stem. The "flowers" will dry out and can then be painted.

An **aquarium** from an empty glass jar – a medium-sized coffee jar is fine, but needs a tight-fitting lid. Make a base of pretty stones and rocks and use a few pipecleaners for twisty water-weeds. Make an octopus from a lump of plasticine and his eight legs from small lengths of pipecleaners. The octopus will float in the aquarium from a discreet piece of string pushed into his body and attached to the underside of the lid at the other end by sticky tape or plasticine. Use food colouring to add to the water.

Another octopus can be made from a sheet of newspaper. Tear the legs like a fringe then join the two sides with a paper-clip. This octopus will look best pinned to the wall with a face drawn and coloured on the front.

For a **fishing game** – cut out fish shapes from card or stiff paper. Attach a hair-grip or paper-clip to each shape. Tie a line on a piece of stick, tie a magnet at the other end, and try your luck.

A **cardboard play house** can be made from big cartons – those which hold refrigerators or washing machines can be begged from department stores. Cut a window or two and a door. If the weather's fine it can go outside and be painted. Or it can be papered with left-over ends of wallpaper or with sheets of fancy wrapping paper, or even with pages torn from magazines. It doesn't, of course, *have* to be a house. Turn the carton on its sides so it is lying lengthways, and it would make a fine tunnel or a cave.

Tuesday

Dressing
Up
Day

Your own throw-aways and jumble will probably form the basis of any dressing-up session. Old bedspreads and curtains can be useful for creating caves, hideouts and tents, as well as clothes. If you can get hold of an old top hat, or of bus driver, engine driver or postman hats, so much the better. Cast off handbags, brief cases, evening bags, stoles, scarves, any bits of fur can be used time and time again for different activities.

FINGER PLAY

Two grand people met in a lane	hold up two index fingers
Bowed most politely and bowed once again	bend fingers to each other
How do you do, and how do you do	bend fingers to each other
And how do you do again.	bend both together

I'm going to Lady Washington's
To get a cup of tea,
And five loaves of gingerbread,
So don't you follow me.

You can always change your face . . . Use a **mask** made from a giant cereal box which can fit over the whole head, cut slits for eyes and mouth and decorate. Or cut away back and top or bottom of a cereal box, decorate the front and attach around the head with hat elastic.

For the decoration use glue, wool, or feathers, and raggedy bits of paper and wood-shavings to give extra effect.

You can make a nose by threading hat elastic through a piece of egg-box, half an empty washing-up liquid bottle or a cream carton.

TWO FACE PLAYS

Walk round here	finger on one side of face
Walk round there	finger on other side of face
Knock on the door	tap nose with finger
Lift up the latch	stroke nose underneath
And walk straight in.	pop finger in mouth
Here sits the Lord Mayor	finger in centre of forehead
Here sit his men	one eye
Here sits the cockadoodle	other eye
Here sits the hen	nose
Here sit the little chickens	fingers on teeth
Here they go in	finger on mouth
Chin chopper chin chopper chin chopper chin.	stroke chin

Paper Carrier-Bag Masks

You need a stout paper carrier-bag without its handles.
You can cut holes for eyes, nose and mouth, and paint
or crayon to suit your taste. If you twist the corners
they will make effective ears. Paper carrier-bag masks
last quite a while.

Beards can be made of wood-shavings, steel wool,
cotton wool, hanks of knitting wool or unravelled
twine or rope – all glued on to a basic beard shape made
of card cut to fit the face of the child. Attach card over
the ears with elastic.

There was an old man called Michael Finnegan
He grew whiskers on his chin-egan,
The wind came out and blew them in again,
Poor old Michael Finnegan, begin again.

And there's nothing better than orange peel when it comes to false and gruesome teeth. (Cut set of teeth in the middle of a quarter segment of peel.)

If you make a basic headband of wide elastic, all kinds of ears can be safely pinned to it. Try a pair of old socks stuffed with paper or old stockings, or you can make a spectacular pair with fringed newspaper or tissue paper.

You can use the same elastic band to pin on artificial flowers for brides and grand occasions.
Two golden syrup tins make an interesting pair of feet and add a few inches as well. Thread string or elastic through holes made half-way up the tin and push the feet through. Wellington boots can be transformed with coloured sticky tape which will wash off easily in warm water.

I can hear my feet go tap, tap, tap,
I can hear my hands go clap, clap, clap,
I can hear my fingers go click, click, click,
But I can't hear my head go –
(nod head three times silently.)

Even fake **jewellery** can be expensive. Macaroni jewellery costs very little. You can thread pieces of macaroni on string or elastic to make earrings, bracelets, necklaces, headbands or rings. Macaroni or pasta comes in all kinds of shapes.

Milk-bottle tops can make badges and brooches. Decorate crowns with milk-bottle tops, pieces of silver paper or coloured sticky paper – even wine gums glued on.

Some children spend all afternoon dressing up – just for the fun of dressing up and admiring the result. Others dress up for action!

Like **playing shops** (an old apron with big pockets is an invitation for shop play).

You can make a shop with large cartons for the counter, or by putting a blanket across two trays. A hoard of old foreign coins is luxury play money, but leaves, clothes pegs, milk-bottle tops, matchsticks or dried beans all make acceptable currency.

The "shop" can sell groceries, with empty grocery boxes, plastic bottles, and used tins; a baker's shop can be filled with goodies made from plasticine or modelling dough (see Monday section for recipe).

You can borrow the family's shoes for a shoe-shop, or make a hardware shop with saucepans, and baking tins, and a few kitchen utensils. Provide lots of newspaper for wrapping up.

Three currant buns in a baker's shop,
Big and round with sugar on the top,
Along came Sally with a penny one day,
Bought a currant bun and took it right away.

Two currant buns in a baker's shop,
Big and round with sugar on the top,
Along came Jenny with a penny one day,
Bought a currant bun and took it right away.

One currant bun in a baker's shop,
Big and round with sugar on the top,
Along came Mary with a penny one day,
Bought a currant bun and took it right away.

No currant buns in the baker's shop,
Big and round with sugar on the top,
Along came Humpty with a penny one day,
No currant buns so he had to go away.

And there is always post offices. A letter-box can be made with a carton (just cut out a slit in the front), paper carrier-bags make mailbags, old envelopes and pieces of paper make the letters, stamps can be drawn on, but a few spare trading stamps are a real luxury. Newspaper sellers need a carrier-bag, a week's old newspapers, a handful of small "change" and a hat.

Most **nurses** seem satisfied with a veil or cap and perhaps some cuffs and a badge, and a "doctor" can do with a jacket of some sort. What really seems to matter is the kit. Endless bandages can be made from strips of old sheet, and second-grade cotton wool for swabs is inexpensive. For a few pence you can buy a plastic 5 cc. syringe from any chemist (don't buy the needle!). This will last much longer than the ones from "toy" doctor kits.

A straightforward **family house** can be made under the kitchen table – if you are prepared to lend a blanket to cover the top and sides – but don't forget you can't use the kitchen or the table! Large cartons can also make houses, with blankets or bedspreads covering their tops. Castles, towers, caves, dens and other hideouts need a bit more room, but again large cartons arranged in various ways can provide the answer.

Out of doors – a large blanket or bedspread hung over the washing line and pegged into the ground along the sides makes a roomy tent.

Characters in **dressing up** tend to be fairly predictable. Most children prefer to "give shows" for their own benefit.

Kings and Queens – old net or heavy curtains pinned around shoulders for robes, cardboard crowns stuck with milk-bottle top jewellery.

Princes – woollen tights, decorated wellington boots with the tops turned over, fancy blouse, ordinary buckled belt with cardboard sword, hat with a tissue or newspaper feather (fold a section of newspaper or tissue paper and fringe with scissors).

Fairies (Good) – attach net curtains to wrists for wings and fasten with safety pin on the shoulders.

It's worth while making a few wands of heavy cardboard tacked to a piece of dowelling. Cover wand with paste and silver glitter.

Fairies (Bad) – black or gloomy-coloured heavy wings attached to wrists; sometimes a piece of outdoor greenery attached to the shoulders gives a spooky effect. A mask over the eyes or over the whole face is an additional help. A tiny quantity of flour in a paper bag makes a very powerful "spell".

There was a princess long ago
Long ago, long ago
There was a princess long ago
Long ago.

And she lived in a big high tower
Long ago, long ago
And she lived in a big high tower
Long ago.

One day a fairy waved her wand
Long ago, long ago
One day a fairy waved her wand
Long ago.

The princess slept for a hundred years
Long ago, long ago
The princess slept for a hundred years
Long ago.

A great big forest grew around,
Long ago, long ago
A great big forest grew around
Long ago.

A gallant prince came riding by
Long ago, long ago
A gallant prince came riding by
Long ago.

He took his sword and cut it down
Long ago, long ago
He took his sword and cut it down
Long ago.

He took her hand to wake her up
Long ago, long ago
He took her hand to wake her up
Long ago.

So everybody's happy now
Happy now, happy now
So everybody's happy now,
Happy now.

Young princesses, princes, heroines or heroes can be transformed into old women and men with one basic cloak (cut out of grown-up jumble overcoat), an old hat with steel wool hair pinned underneath brim and pipecleaner spectacles. Remove cloak, hat/hair and spectacles and presto!

Most traditional *villains* will use the false teeth and beards already described. You can also make them fatter by adding a pillow back and front and securing with a belt.

Present-day villains include robots made from one large box fitted over the head and shoulders of the child with pieces of egg-box glued on to the front to make an instrument panel. A cereal-box mask will serve for the head.

Creatures from outer space can be made with apple-box dividers strapped over the shoulders; fit hands and feet into smaller cartons and boxes. A kitchen colander stuck with various greenery makes impressive headgear. Crêpe paper is still very good value for making hats, bows, sashes and long streamers.

Here is a rocket that flew to the moon.

Here is a man, Professor McSpoon,
Who constructed the rocket that flew to the moon.

Here is Billy, who asked for a ride,
In the moonrocket. "Certainly, come inside,"
Said the clever inventor, Professor McSpoon,
Who constructed the rocket that flew to the moon.

Here goes the blast-off, buzzing and fizzing,
As into the sky the rocket goes whizzing
With Billy, the boy who asked for a ride
In the moonrocket, crouching and clinging inside,
With the clever inventor, Professor McSpoon
Who constructed the rocket that flew to the moon.

Here is the moon, placid and white,
Shining peacefully down that night,
When the blast-off went banging and buzzing and fizzing,
As into the sky the rocket went whizzing,
With Billy, the boy who asked for a ride
In the moonrocket, crouching and clinging inside,
With the clever inventor, Professor McSpoon,
Who constructed the rocket that flew to the moon.

Here is the rocket, in orbit, then landing,
The Professor and Billy climb out and are standing
At last on the moon, which, placid and white,
Was shining peacefully down that night
When the blast-off went banging and buzzing and fizzing,
As into the sky the rocket went whizzing
With Billy, the boy who asked for a ride
In the moonrocket, crouching and clinging inside
With the clever inventor, Professor McSpoon,
Who constructed the rocket that flew to the moon.

The One Man Band. He can have a hooter made from an empty cardboard tube in his mouth or a conventional whistle. One saucepan lid on a string hanging over his shoulder and one in his hand. His drumstick is held in the other – a wooden spoon is fine – and as he beats alternate drums he blows his hooter. If you can spare some plastic cups with handles a bracelet can be made and fixed around his hand or his ankle, and every so often he can stand still and shake away!

A Hobby-Horse. If knights or robbers need a horse for a quick get-away, a broomstick with a sock or a very large wellington boot pulled over the end of the handle will serve. Tie a ribbon round its "neck".

Magicians' Cloaks can be made from grown-up size overcoats (jumble variety). Glue a few stars and moons on the hem, make the hat with a cone of stiff paper to fit the head, and decorate. If the child is small enough and the cloak big enough, endless things can be hidden to produce the required magical effect. After all, it's all in the word – if you say abracadabra and produce the egg whisk – that's magic by anybody's standards.

You can make a **toy theatre** (using dolls, bears and stuffed toys as cast) from a large carton and pieces of cardboard. Cut an entrance either side of the carton and make a curtain with material taped or tacked to a baton which can be "lifted" or "dropped" in front of the set. Make scenery from pictures painted on to pieces of card, which are dropped into the back of the carton. If the production is "Goldilocks", for example, a woodland scene, a kitchen scene and a bedroom scene might be required.

Wednesday

growing living things day

Spring is a time to watch things growing.

A pie-plate garden. Use an old pie-plate or a foil baking dish and cover the bottom with small stones or pieces of broken flower pot. Put in some soil, then make a jungle garden by planting weeds. Water every so often and watch them grow. Hairy monster crabs and pipe-cleaner people can live very happily in such a garden.

You can grow beans on blotting-paper soaked with water, or put slices of carrot tops in water – after a few days the carrot tops will sprout a "fern". Put a seed potato in a yoghurt carton and cover the top. Make a few round holes in the sides of the carton and watch the potato sprouts curl out of the holes towards the light. You can grow mustard and cress in a yoghurt carton and paint a face on the outside. When the green "hair" begins to grow, cut it and eat it for tea.

You can sow the letters of your name in mustard and cress seed in wet blotting paper and watch it grow.

SOME STORIES ABOUT WILD FLOWERS

A dandelion is called a dandelion because its leaves look like sharp lion's teeth.

A daisy is called a daisy because people used to think it looked like "the day's eye". When the sun rose in the morning its petals opened like an eye and when the sun went down at night its petals closed and the "eye" went to sleep.

FORGET-ME-NOTS

There's a story that a princess was walking by the banks of a stream and saw some pretty blue flowers growing near the water. She asked a kind knight to pick some for her and so he went down to the stream and picked her a bunch. But, alas, he fell into the water and could not swim. As he was carried along by the stream with the flowers in his hand he called to the Princess "Forget-me-not! Forget-me-not".

How many puffs
To tell the time
From this fat, fluffy
Dandelion?

Lift your pretty chin
Look up into the sky
Yes! You do like butter
Now you tell me why!

A **Wormery**. Parks and gardens should supply you with enough worms in the spring to make a wormery. Put garden soil into a glass jar with two or three large worms near the bottom. Then put a layer of sand and a layer of wet, decaying leaves. Put brown paper round the sides of the jar and keep the soil damp. After a week, remove the brown paper, and a pattern of tunnels and paths will be marked in the sand where the worms have moved upwards towards the leaves. Then let the worms go . . .

Today I saw a little worm,
Wriggling on his belly,
Perhaps he'd like to come inside,
And see what's on the telly!

An **Easter Tree** is easy to make with a piece of dead branch. Paint it white and when it's dry you can make different kinds of birds to sit in the tree. Make them with feathers scrounged from park or garden, either stick them into corks, or twist them into pipe-cleaners. Tie them on the branches with cotton or wool. Scraps of material make wings which can be glued on to a cardboard body and put in the branches. You can decorate the rest of the tree with milk-bottle tops and twists of tissue paper. In the middle of the tree you can make a nest of straw or grass. You can make big eggs with ping-pong balls or small ones from marbles. Cover both kinds with pretty paper, sweet papers, silver paper or tissue.

Spring skies produce a variety of clouds and the changeable weather sometimes makes sense of old weather rhymes.
You can't always be wrong!

Mackerel sky!
Mackerel sky!
Never long wet,
Never long dry.

If the oak is out before the ash,
Then you may expect a splash.
If the ash is out before the oak,
Then you can expect a soak.

Red at night,
Shepherd's delight,
Red in the morning,
Shepherds take warning.

If the rooks build high
The weather will be dry.

A WEATHER RIDDLE

Red and blue and delicate green,
The King can't catch it and neither can the Queen,
Pull it in the room and you can catch it soon,
Answer this riddle by tomorrow at noon.
Answer: *A rainbow.*

Spring is also the time for new babies!

FINGER PLAY

Our fat black cat	one fist
Has five new kittens	Hold five fingers up on other hand
Because she loves them	
They fit round her like mittens.	fit fingers over fist
Sssh! Sssh! Sssh!	
They're all asleep.	
We'll have one quick look	
And away we'll creep.	

And of course a really fool-proof way of telling which way the wind is blowing never comes amiss!

In the **summer** parks and gardens can supply daisies for chains, but lots of other flowering weeds can look just as good. A dandelion chain is easier to make (the stalks are that much thicker) and the results can be effective. If you can find them, white convolvulus make pretty garlands and also provide the raw material for making poor old granny "Hop out of bed!"

Granny, hop . . .
Granny, hop . . .
Granny, hop out of bed!

With antirrhinums you can also make the dragon snap!

Snippetty,
Snippetty,
SNAP *goes the dragon,*
SNAP! SNAP!

And you can make pea-pods go pop!

Five porky peas in a pea-pod pressed,
One grew, two grew, and so did all the rest,
They grew and they grew and they didn't stop,
Until one day the pod went pop!

Very often small children will carefully collect a posy of
flowers consisting solely of flower heads and no stems!
Utilise the collection in a floating flower bowl. Add a
walnut shell or a leaf boat or two.

Hollyhock ladies can twirl in fingers or float sedately in
a lake. Join a fully-blown hollyhock flower and a bud
by a cocktail stick. The bud is the head. If the lady
needs arms, another stick can be pushed through the
centre of the bud.

Two or three small sprays of beech leaves tied together
at the ends make a very cooling and elegant fan.

Flower pictures can be made from garden flowers and weeds.

On a sheet of stout paper, outline the sky, grass, hedgerow and tree-trunk. Pierce holes in the paper and stick bits of grass, flowers, leaves etc. through the holes to create a collage effect for branches, shrubs and flowers. Stick the stems of the grasses and leaves on to the back of the picture with sticky tape.

A yoghurt carton, a small magnifying-glass and a pair of tweezers form the essentials for a basic bug-hunting kit. A small collection of ants, ladybirds, spiders and grubs of various kinds can be kept and observed for a few hours. It seems that half the interest is in first catching them gently, looking at them, and then returning them to their natural home.

Snails, on the other hand, can provide hours of amusement and don't need to be moved out of their environment. You can improve the environment and add some entertainment by adding a few long sticks or stones, and provided there are enough snails a miniature circus can be established – or if two can be found a race of sorts can be run.

If caterpillars are collected and kept it's a good idea to put their food in a small jar of water inside the box. This way the leaves keep fresh for longer. It takes a lot of patience to keep a caterpillar long enough to form a chrysalis, but it can be worth it. Once the chrysalis is formed, keep the box in a dark, cool place.

"Who's that tickling my back?" said the wall.
"Me," said a small caterpillar,
"I'm learning to crawl."

Flutter your eye,
Like a butterfly,
Flutter by . . .
Flutter by . . .
Flutter by . . .

A PUDDING TO CELEBRATE MIDSUMMER'S DAY

You need:

    One sponge fruit flan case

    One packet of raspberry jelly

    A few strawberries and one piece of apple

Prepare jelly and set solid.

Put the strawberries in the flan and the piece of apple Then break up the jelly and pile the pieces over the strawberry and apple. They must be completely hidden by the jelly.

When the host or hostess comes to serve the flan, he or she should be seemingly or genuinely unaware where the piece of apple is. Whoever receives it is entitled to a wish – but he or she mustn't wish until they've shared the apple!

A plate of cherries can be demolished while playing "Tommy".
One player leaves the room while the others decide which cherry is "Tommy". When the player returns he tries to guess which cherry is Tommy. If he is right he can eat it – someone else has a turn, and so it goes on. When the cherries are all eaten everybody's future can be told with the stones.

Tinker, tailor,
Soldier sailor,
Rich man, poor man,
Beggar man, thief!

I will learn to ride a two-wheeler . . . or get married . . .

This year,
Next year,
Sometime,
Never!

I will be married in . . .

Silk, satin,
Cotton, rags.

A SUMMER WEATHER RIDDLE
I washed my hands in water
That was never rained or run
I dried them with a towel
That was never wove nor spun.

Answer: *The Dew and the Sun.*

Autumn is conker time!
Iddy Iddy onker
My first conker
Iddy Iddy ack,
My first smack!

With patience and some adult help, conkers can make
excellent necklaces. If they are painted with clear nail
varnish they will shine for longer.

Bulb Planting

If hyacinth bulbs are grown in water in wide-necked bottles such as salad cream jars the whole growth of leaves, roots and flowers can be watched. Roots remain white but the leaves turn green and it is fun to guess what colour the flower will be. To prevent the bulb being knocked off the rim of the bottle, put it in a ring of plasticine. The base of the bulb should just touch the water.

Yoghurt cartons make very successful flower-pots for crocus bulbs grown in fibre. Keep the pots in a dark cupboard until the buds are well-formed and then bring them into the light.

Harvest time in the city doesn't show very much but . . .

Oh mother dear,
I sadly fear
My appetite
Is always here!

Everything needs food!
A large oak-tree in full leaf gets through a ton of water a day!
A blue tit gets through 1,500 grubs a day!
Moles are not fussy . . . they will eat anything they find underneath the ground . . . even newspaper!
A bird like a stork can go shopping for its food. Its big beak can take in a frog or two, a fish, some insects. It packs the lot in and flies back to its family and its nest.
And a brand-new baby sometimes drinks a pint and a half of milk a day!

SOME AUTUMN ANIMALS
Acorns, pine cones, autumn leaves, branches and twigs can be made into a whole menagerie of animals . . .

Birds may be flying to warmer countries but flocks of sycamore birds are around – one sycamore seed with a berry fastened to it with a matchstick or cocktail stick.

And the conker bird – one conker in its shell. . . . Make long legs with pieces of twig, string some berries on wire for his neck, and add a big berry for his head.

And the pine-cone owl – one pine-cone is the head and body. A couple of pieces of feathery evergreen held with plasticine make the wings.

Autumn nights produce batches of shooting-stars
worth watching for . . . But then the sky on any clear
night is a source of wonder.

Star light
Star bright
First star I've seen tonight,
Wish I may
Wish I might
Have the wish I wish tonight.

And the harvest moon of course.

I see the moon
And the moon sees me
God bless the moon
And God bless me!

Winter is the time to feed the birds.

A BIRD PUDDING

Mix together some small pieces of bread, chunks of apple peel and a few nuts, and bind with melted lard. Prepare a cream carton by making a hole in the base and threading a string through it, securing it with a knot. Fill the prepared carton with the mixture and when the fat is set the pudding should be hard and firm enough to be hung outside a window or from a tree.

A WINTER RIDDLE
A milk-white bird
Floats down through the air,
And never a tree
But he lights there
Answer: *Snow*

Clear frosty nights can produce icicles – but they're not always accessible. You can try making your own with these rather odd ingredients: one old sock, one plastic bottle.
Basically, you need dripping water.
Fill the bottle, but wrap the sock around it so that the water inside the bottle doesn't freeze. Lay the bottle on its side and at an angle which will produce dripping water. Leave it outside on a balcony or a window-ledge on a very cold night – and the weather should do the rest.
You can try adding food flavouring to the water. This can make a green or a red icicle.

A miniature skating rink for toy cars can be made by freezing water outside in a baking dish or pan. Car races become quite exciting as the ice begins to break up, and another ice rink can always be made the next night if the weather holds.

A big winter cooking apple and five small potatoes can be stuck together with cocktail sticks to make a roly-poly man.
Whichever way he goes – he rolls! Sometimes on his head . . . sometimes on one leg.

Small pieces of branch and dead twig can be collected to make simple decorations for Christmas.
Dab the branches with cellulose filler, mixed to a thick paste, or make a picture of plaster of paris, then sprinkle glitter over them.

Four Sundays before Christmas is the time to start lighting the Advent Ring.
The easiest way to make the Advent Ring is to put four lumps of plasticine in a deep soup-plate or shallow bowl, and stick white household candles in each. Fill the bowl with sprigs of evergreen, baubles and decorations. Each Sunday the children take it in turns to light and put out the candles – and if they're put out after an hour or so they will last the four Sundays.
Remember the birds on Christmas Day!

Thursday

Ideas
Day

Some ideas for **picture-making.**

Very many ordinary household things can be pasted onto a stiffish piece of paper or card to make pictures. For the background you need a fairly thick mixture of wallpaper paste, and if you add a few dollops of powder colour it will be more effective.

Try:

Lentils, rice, macaroni, pieces of spaghetti.

String, wool, twine, wood-shavings.

Pieces of fabric, paper doilies, cotton wool.

Water melon seeds, leaves, twigs, seed-heads.

Pieces of drinking straws, pipecleaners.

Small stones, shells, pieces of egg-shell, buttons.

You can make patterns in a paste-and-colour-powder mixture with strips of stiff card, old pencils, empty cotton reels, a wooden spoon handle, the back of a spoon, the prongs of a fork, the different surfaces of an empty matchbox.

And of course there's painting with your fingers! Try it on a washable surface . . . like a laminated table top or linoleum floor. Or use stiff card or paper. Use a mixture of thick powder paint, and add some paste.

Every part of your hand makes a different pattern.
Start with the finger-tips, make them wriggle through
the paint.
Then each finger.
Then the thumb and the palm of the hand. Roll them
round and round.
Try using your wrists, thump them up and down in the
paint.
If you want to make some prints of the picture, lightly
press clean paper over the patterns. Several prints can
usually be made from one picture.
Try making prints on clean paper with: potatoes cut
across into halves, half an orange or lemon, pieces of
foam rubber or sponge, empty cotton reels. Dip the
surfaces in thick, bright colours and stamp them on the
paper.
Dip a length of string in some thick paint and let it
trail across clean paper into swirls and whirls of paint.
Or put a splodge of paint in the centre of the paper and
blow the paint into patterns and shapes with a drinking
straw.

Music makes patterns too.
Just turn on the radio and listen. Let the paintbrush,
crayon or pencil move over the paper with the music.
Or you can "draw" shapes in the air for fun!

Reach up and paint the ceiling
Reach round and paint the walls
Reach over and paint the window-sills
Reach down and paint the floor
Reach out and paint the chimney-pots
Now get a little tiddly brush and do the corners!

Some ideas for making music . . .

Oh, we can play on the big bass drum
And this is the music to it!
Boom! Boom! Boom!
Goes the big bass drum
And that's the way we do it!

Three easy drums.
Empty saucepan with wooden spoon.
Cocoa tin with string held in place by lid.
Plastic bucket covered with stiff brown paper tied on
securely. Pat with the fingers for a tom-tom effect.
A slightly grander drum.
An empty paint tin with both ends removed. Cover each
end with old inner tube or rubber sheeting. Punch holes
in the rubber, and thread shoe-laces or cord through
for the cross-over laces.

And of course you can tap out a fine rhythm with hands and feet. Turn on the radio and try.

Oh, we can play on the piccolo
And this is the music to it!
Tootle, tootle, tootle
Goes the piccolo
And that's the music to it!

Some things to blow.

Cover one end of an empty paper-towel roll with grease-proof paper. Punch a few holes along the top and blow! Use your fingers over the holes to vary the sounds. Cover a comb with tissue paper. Blow and hum against the paper and it will make a sound like a harmonica.

Have a blow, Jo!
Go on Jo!
Have a blow!
Blow as high
And as low
As you can go, Jo!
Go on Jo!
Have a blow!

Or just hum your favourite tune and tap your fingers against your lips as you march along.

Oh, we can play on the tambourine
And this is the music to it!
Rattle, rattle shake
Goes the tambourine
And that's the way we do it!

Shakers and rattlers.
Empty yoghurt cartons can be stuck together with
sticky tape and filled with rice, beans, macaroni, lentils,
gravel.
Washing-up liquid bottles can also be used, and a piece
of dowelling can be jammed into the neck to make
a handle.
Empty tins and boxes filled with small stones or buttons
make good impromptu rattles. Make sure the lids are
fastened tightly!

A small amount of water in a tin sloshed and slurped
with enthusiasm is another variation.
Leaves collected in the autumn and put in a paper bag
with the end tied tightly onto a piece of dowelling
make a pleasant swishing kind of rattle.
And of course you can always shake, rattle and roll
around yourself.

Try this to the tune of "*She'll be coming round the mountain!*"

Oh I'm shaking like a jelly on a plate
Oh I'm shaking like a jelly on a plate
Oh I'm shaking like a jelly
Like a flippy floppy jelly
Oh I'm shaking like a jelly on a plate!

Oh I'm rattling like a bean in a frying-pan
Oh I'm rattling like a bean in a frying-pan
Oh I'm rattling like a bean
A rattle-tattle bean
Oh I'm rattling like a bean in a frying-pan!

Oh I'm rolling like a pumpkin down a hill
Oh I'm rolling like a pumpkin down a hill
Oh I'm rolling like a pumpkin
A roly-poly pumpkin
I'm rolling like a pumpkin down a hill!

Different things make different sounds. You can make
up a story using sounds for some of the words . . .
One day it was . . . (pitter-patter-pitter) and a big fat . . .
(miaow, miaow) had nothing to do except sit inside and
feel sorry for himself and . . . (growl, growl, growl).
So he turned on the radio and he heard . . . (la-la-la,
la-la-la!). So he began to . . . (one-two-three tap! tap!)
and he began to . . . (la-la-la, tirra-boomdeday la-la-la!)
as well.
And all the people came out of their houses into the
pouring . . . (pitter-patter-pitter) and stood outside his
windows and listened to the . . . (la-la-la, one-two-three
tap! tap! la-la-la, tirra-boomdeday la-la-la!).
And when the big fat . . . (miaow, miaow) had finished,
they all . . . (clap, clap) and . . . (hurrah, hurrah!). And
gave three big cheers for the caterwauling cat!

Or you can play a guessing game with sounds . . .
One player leaves the room or closes his eyes while the
other uses different household objects to make a noise
with. It could be: rolling a cotton reel across a table,
whizzing an egg beater, tapping a spoon against a cup,
banging two spoons together.

Or you can make lots of sounds into a song. Like the
one about Suzanna.

There was an old farmer had an old sow (SNORT) *how*
(GRUNT) *how* (WHISTLE) *idily dow*

CHORUS
Suzanna's a funiful man (SNORT) *an* (GRUNT) *and*
(WHISTLE) *idily dan,*
Suzanna's a funiful man.
Sing laslie go rings a rillo,
Suzanna's a funiful man (SNORT) *an* (GRUNT) *an*
(WHISTLE) *idily dan,*
Suzanna's a funiful man.

Now this old sow had some little pigs – (SNORT) *igs*
(GRUNT) *igs* (WHISTLE) *idily digs*

Now these little pigs they had some clean straw (SNORT)
aw (GRUNT) *aw* (WHISTLE) *idily daw*

Now these little pigs they muddled their muck (SNORT)
uck (GRUNT) *uck* (WHISTLE) *idily uck*

Now these little pigs they had curly tails (SNORT) *ails*
(GRUNT) *ails* (WHISTLE) *idily dails*

Now these little pigs they had to be stuck (SNORT) *usk*
(GRUNT) *usk* (WHISTLE) *idily duck*

Now these little pigs they made some nice ham (SNORT)
am (GRUNT) *am* (WHISTLE) *idily dam*

Now these little pigs they made the best bacon (SNORT)
acon (GRUNT) *acon* (WHISTLE) *idily dacon*

Now these little pigs they grunted no more (SNORT) *ore*
(GRUNT) *ore* (WHISTLE) *idily dore.*

Sometimes it's an idea to tidy up!

The Workshop You can sort out different kinds and
sizes of screws into boxes. And nuts and bolts and nails
as well. If you use a kitchen tray to work on they won't
get lost.

The Button-Box Use an egg-box to sort out all the
different sizes of buttons. Maybe you can also go
through old clothes looking for buttons to add to the
button-box.

Sometimes old clothes and linen can do with tearing up
to make into dusters and rags.

If there are old nylon stockings in the rag bag three of
them can be tied onto a door handle and used to
practise plaiting.

The cutlery drawer and the vegetable rack provide more
opportunities for a good tidy-up!

Washing, cleaning and polishing – especially washing
down paint-work with a sponge and a little water – *can*
produce commendable results!

Sometimes it's interesting to turn things the wrong
way round . . .

From an old magazine cut out pictures of people . . . go
through the magazine again and cut out pictures of
shoes, hats, handbags, furniture, flowers. Mix them up
and paste together some nonsense people and things.

If my shoes are on my hands
Can I clap?
If my gloves are on my feet
Can I walk?
If my coat's the wrong way round
Am I going out?
Or coming in?
If my specs drop off my nose
Can I see you with my chin?

I'm a little teapot, short and stout,
Here's my handle, here's my spout
When I see the teacups hear me shout
Tip me up and pour me out!

I'm a big beech tree
In the warm, warm summer
And I'm growing, I'm growing
The wind is moving in my green,
green leaves
And I'm rustling, I'm rustling
There's a bird on my branch
And another one too
And they're singing, they're
singing
And high up in the blue
There's a golden sun
And it's shining, its shining!

THE BEAR HUNT

I want to go on a bear hunt.
All right! Let's go! (Slap thighs with hands)
Oh look! There's a brook.
Can't go round it! (make "go round" motion with hand)
Can't go under it! (make "go under" motion with hand)
Can't go over it! (make "go over" motion with hand)
Got to go through it!
All right!
Let's go! (make swimming moves)
Oh look!
There's a bridge
Can't go round it! (make "go round" motion with hands)
Can't go under it! (make "go under" motion with hands)
Got to go over it!
All right!
Let's go! (Thump hands on chest as you go over bridge)

Oh look!
There's a swamp
Can't go round it! (make "go round" motion with ha
Can't go under it! (make "go under" motion with ha
Can't go over it! (make "go over" motion with han
Got to go through it!
All right!
Let's go! (Slide hands together)

Oh look!
There's a tree
Can't go over it! (make "go over" motion with hands)
Can't go under it! (make "go under" motion with hands)
Got to go up it!
All right! (make movements with hands for
Let's go! climbing tree)

Oh look!
There's a cave
Let's go and see
What's inside?
All right!
Let's go!   (Tramp softly and lower voices for
                       next lines)

Let's go softly
Let's go quietly

Oh look!
I see two big eyes
I see two big paws
I feel something like a fur coat
It looks like a bear
It feels like a bear
IT IS A BEAR!   (loudly)
Let's go!   (Tramp fast with feet)
Up the tree   (make fast motions up the tree)
Down the tree   (make fast motions climbing down the
                       tree)
Through the swamp (make fast motions, sliding hands)
Over the bridge   (thump chest)
Swim the brook   (make fast swimming motions)
Down the street   (tramp fast)
Open the gate   (open gate)
In the door,
shut it fast   (slam door)
PHEWWWWWW!

Jump-jump! Kangaroo Brown,
Jump-jump! Off to town
Jump-jump! Up hill and down
Jump-jump! Kangaroo Brown!

Jack-in-a-box
Is a funny old man
He hides in his box
As small as he can
He hides in his box
As small as he can
Then SUDDENLY OUT
he jumps!
UP! DOWN UP! DOWN
Funny Jack-in-a-box.

I'm the man
With the wellington boots
That stomps and stomps and stomps and stomps
And stomps and stomps and stomps and stomps
Until he gets back home

And when he gets back home
He stomps and stomps and stomps and stomps
And stomps and stomps and stomps and stomps
Until he finds his slippers

And when he finds his slippers
He pitters and patters and patters and pitters
And patters and pitters and pitters and patters
Until he finds his paper.

And when he's found his paper he sits down on the sofa
and has a good read!

Some people to be . . .

OLD MRS STUCK-IN-THE-MUD
Both boots stuck in the mud,
Both feet stuck in the boots,
Both feet stuck to my legs,
Both legs stuck to me,
HELP!
I'm old Mrs Stuck-in-the-Mud!

MISS GLORIA GRAND
Miss Gloria Grand got ready for the dance,
She did her eyelashes,
Painted her mouth,
(Very carefully, no splodges)
Powdered her nose,
Combed her long, long hair
Put on her earrings,
Fastened her necklace,
Stepped into her grand, gold-buckled shoes,
Picked up her long swishy skirts,
Opened her door
AND
Tripped over the milk-bottles!
CRASH! BANG! SPLASH.
(she wasn't hurt – but she had to start all over again!)

MRS SLAM-BANG

Mrs *Slam-bang* stamped *down the stairs*
And slammed *on her hat*
And stamped *into her boots*
And heaved *open the door*
And slam-banged *the door shut*
And slam-bang, slam-banged *all*
The way down the street to catch her bus.
And when she caught her bus
Everybody went
Phew!
Thank goodness Mrs Slam-bang's gone to work
Now we can have some peace.

FACES

Johnny Brown had a frown
Can you frown like Johnny Brown?
Mary Crimper had a simper
Can you simper like Mary Crimper?
Hetty Hope had a mope
Can you mope like Hetty Hope?
But Lily Lyle had the brightest smile
Can you smile like Lily Lyle?

Or can you make a picture of yourself – just as you are!
Get a double sheet of newspaper and lie down flat on
top of it.
Get someone to draw round your shape with a crayon.
Then you can cut yourself out!

Some ideas for games inside.
Statues All you need is the radio and someone to turn it
off and on. When the music stops you must freeze like
a statue until the music starts again.
You can use the radio too, for playing "Last Man
Down". When the music stops you must sit down
quickly – Last Man Down has to take the next turn
operating the radio.

Guessing the Nursery Rhyme You can act out Humpty
Dumpty, Little Miss Muffet or any nursery rhyme and
everybody else can guess which it is.

Keep Moving! One person starts by clapping their
hands, then the next must clap their hands and add
something else – touching their toes perhaps – and so
on for as long as possible.

Mirrors Stand or sit opposite someone and try and do
everything your opposite does at the same time.

Stunts Can you rub your stomach with one hand and
pat your head at the same time?
Now try it round the other way!
Can you make a "3" in the air with one hand and an
"O" with the other hand at the same time?
Can you sing *Ba Ba Black Sheep* while someone else
sings *Twinkle, Twinkle, Little Star*?

A song to do as well as sing!

Let's all clap together,
Clap together, clap together.
Let's all clap together Clap! Clap! Clap!
Clap, clap this a-away
Clap, clap that a-away
Clap, clap all the day

Let's all cry together,
Cry together, cry together
Let's all cry together, cry, cry, cry.
Cry, cry this a-away
Cry, cry that a-away
Cry, cry all the day
Boo! Hoo! Hoo!

Let's all laugh together,
Laugh together, laugh together,
Let's all laugh together, Ha-Ha-Ha
Ha Ha this a-away
Ha Ha that a-away
Ha-Ha all the day
Ha! Ha! Ha!

Some ideas for out of doors.

The Wibbly Wobbly game is best played out of doors.
The Wibbly Wobbly line is made from chalk along a
path or you can use leaves or pieces of stick. It doesn't
matter how long or short it is but it has to wibble and
wobble. Then you try to walk the line, heel to toe,
without falling over. One can play against himself, or
two against each other.

THE WIBBLY WOBBLY WALK
Oh we all dance the wibbly wobbly walk
All talk the wibbly wobbly talk
All smile the wibbly wobbly smile
And wink at all the pretty girls
With wibbly wobbly eyes
Oh we all laugh the wibbly wobbly laugh
Till the day is dawning
And because of the wibbly wobbly night
We get the wibbly wobbly feeling in the morning.

Cleaning up the toys and bikes is a useful outdoor
activity.
A big bowl of soapy water will wash all the doll's
bedclothes and clothes, clean the toy cars, wash down
tricycles, scooters and leave some for bubble blowing
as well.

Friday

Experiment Day

Air is all around you.

Take a deep breath and fill your lungs with air.

Put your fingers on your ribs and feel the air in your lungs.

Blow out the air and feel your ribs pushing the air out of your lungs.

Hold your fingers up to your mouth as you breathe out and feel the air tickle them.

Blow into a paper bag – and screw up the neck. Does the air stay inside?

See what else has air inside it.

Try dropping a small clod of earth into a glass of water . . . you'll see some bubbles. That means there's air in the earth.

Now try dropping a pebble in the water. Any air in the pebble?

Try blowing some air through a drinking straw . . .

Can you blow the pages of a newspaper, the pages of a magazine or the pages of a book? Which is the easiest to blow?

Blow into some water with the drinking straw and the air will make bubbles.

If you put some oil in the water the air can't turn into bubbles so easily – see what happens when you blow into some oily water.

Some shapes can move through the air faster than others . . . try a flat sheet of paper and a crumpled sheet of paper. Drop both of them from the same height at the same time and see which hits the ground first.

Water . . . at the kitchen sink.

What will float on water?

Try a bottle top, a penny, a cork, a piece of paper, an empty plastic bottle, a spoon.

Which of them floats best?

Which of them sank to the bottom first?

Try filling some paper cake-cases with sugar-lumps. See which sugar-lump boat sinks to the bottom first.

Which soaks up water better? A piece of sponge or foam rubber or a piece of cardboard?

Try making some striped celery. Put a few fresh sticks of celery in a tumbler of water with some cochineal added to the water. After a while the celery will drink up the water and you'll have candy-striped celery.

What happens to a piece of cardboard if you leave it in water for a long time?

What happens to a pebble if you leave it in water for a long time?

Does your hand look different when you put it under the water?

Try putting a pencil in a glass of water. Does it look a different shape?

Fill some tumblers with different levels of water, tap the rim of the tumblers with a spoon and listen to the different sounds.

Those little ticks of time,
Keep on tocking, tocking, tocking, tocking,
Tic-a-tick-a-tic-tic-tocking all the day,
But those little ticks of time
Know no reason, know no rhyme.
They just tick-a-tick-a-tic-tick-tock the time away.

The sun picks up little drops of water
From the sea as she rolls around the sky
When her hands are full endowed,
She makes a little cloud
And sends the little cloud drifting by.
The little cloud goes drifting through the heavens,
He has a little task he must fulfil.
He makes little water balls and gently lets them fall
As raindrops down upon the hill.

As the raindrops fall upon the hilltop
Each one stops to say hello,
And their faces fairly beam as they make a little stream
And the little stream goes trickling down below.

The stream meets another and another,
And they come upon another running free,
And they gurgle as they run and all become as one
Mighty river flowing to the sea.

Choose your raindrop – see which one gets to the window-sill first.

Try drawing a picture with a white wax crayon and then painting over the surface with water paint. Will the paint cover the wax?
Will it mix with the wax?
What *will* mix with water?
Put a spoonful of sugar in a teacup of cold water and then try some in warm water. Does the sugar change the water at all? Put a little sand in some water. Does it mix well? Does it change the water at all?
You can try salad oil, butter, a drop of tomato ketchup, a teaspoon of salt in teacups of cold water and warm water and see which mixes best.
What do you think gets dirt off your hands quickest – cold water or warm water and a little soap?

Weighing and measuring

You can make a pair of scales with a plank of wood
(a ruler will do) placed on a small box or a block.
See if you can get the ruler to balance different weights.
Try a potato one end and a cotton-reel the other. Which
one is the heavier?
Try something big like an orange or an apple and find
a lot of small things to balance the other end like
peanuts, or small stones or raisins. Try balancing
yourself. Stand up and put all your weight on one foot
and then the other. See if you can stay upright or if
you fall over.

Measure some steps. Put one foot in front of the other
and walk and count. How many steps does it take to
cross your bedroom, or go round the living-room, or
go across the kitchen? Or right round the garden?

Some experiments with cooking Take a tablespoon of margarine and two tablespoons of sugar and mix them up. Keep mixing and beating them together and see what kind of mixture they turn into.

Take two tablespoons of flour and a teaspoon of margarine and mix them up. You won't get far with a spoon so try rubbing them together with your fingers and see what kind of mixture they turn into.
See if you can separate the yolk of an egg from the white. Beat up the white with a whisk and see how stiff and frothy you can get it. If you fold in a little sugar and some Rice Krispies this makes a very good mixture to bake in the oven.
Try soaking some raisins in water overnight.
See if they've changed at all in the morning.
Try lentils, dried peas and beans as well.

Experiments with your **senses**

Your eyes, your hands, your nose, your tongue, your ears, all tell you what things look, feel, smell, taste and sound like, and your brain tells you their names.
So try putting a whole lot of things on a table or a tray and, with your eyes closed, guessing what they are. Sometimes you'll have to use your nose to smell them out, sometimes your hands to feel them, sometimes you'll have to listen to them.

Sometimes you can hear things better if you put "your ear to the ground" like the Red Indians used to. Next time you're outside, try listening for someone coming with your ear to the ground.
Or you can do it at the kitchen table. Get someone to lightly scratch the surface of the table. So lightly that you can't hear it . . . then put your ear on the table and find out if you can hear it like that.

What makes a reflection? A mirror makes a good one,
but try looking at yourself in some other shiny surfaces:
the back of a spoon, a shiny brass door handle.

A magnifying-glass can make all sorts of things look
different.
Try using one on grains of sugar, flowers, leaves, dust
in a corner, your fingernails, the palm of your hand and
the ball of your thumb, a piece of material. If you look
at your jersey, your socks and your shirt or dress you
can see all the different ways the threads are put
together to make the cloth.
A magnet attracts metal Run a magnet over yourself
and see if you are wearing any metal. Take it round the
garden or through the park and see if you can find any
metal there.
If it's a very strong magnet it will make some metal
things jump . . . try putting some nails on a piece of
cardboard and running the magnet along underneath.
Do the nails jump about?

Some good places to **visit** and find out what's going on there!

A building site If there is a very tall block of flats or office block being erected, the contractors will be using a crane. See how they build the tall building around the crane. Why do they do that? How do they get the crane out?

Look for the site hut and see if you can see one of the builders making the tea for everybody.

Look at the builders' big boots and their donkey jackets with the patches of leather over the shoulders. Sometimes they wear safety helmets.

A Tobacconist or Paper Kiosk How does the man *get in* there? See if you can find the door!

The Post-box If there's one near where you live – make a note of the time the van comes to collect the letters. It's printed on the outside of the box. Then go back and watch the postman empty the letters into his mailbag. Look for his big bunch of keys. How do you think he knows which one to use on that post-box?

The Hospital If you live near one take a walk past sometime. You might see someone in bed that would like to be waved to . . . you might see nurses and doctors going in and out of the doors. Hospital porters wheeling chairs and trolleys with patients – see how carefully they do it!

Fish and Chip Shop Next time you're buying fish and chips see if you can find the big dish or bucket of batter the fish is dipped in before it is fried.

What do you think batter is made of?

Road mending Next time you pass some road-menders, watch out for a pneumatic presser! See if you can jump like that!

Drapery Store You can watch the assistants roll the cloth off the bolts and spread it along the counter. See how straight they can cut with their scissors. Sometimes they wear their scissors on a special belt around their waists. New cloth smells good.

Banks and Post Offices are good places to watch people counting money very quickly. You try with some paper when you get home – or some pennies or buttons.

In the bus coming home Watch how the conductor works his ticket machine. In a double-decker, watch him use the mirror to see that the passengers are safely aboard.

Piles of golden oranges,
Grapes both black and green.
Pyramids of apples
And the biggest plums you've seen.
Earthy brown potatoes,
Cauliflowers and sprouts,
People push and jostle
Everybody shouts.

Stalls are getting empty,
Barrows wheeled away,
Have we bought enough to last
Until next market day?

Every Day is Story Day

Play School has a story in every programme. They range from picture books to stories told by visitors about ordinary everyday events.

In the same way, no doubt, your own experiences often form the basis for a story. "How I Got Stuck in the Lift" may well prove more riveting than the most glossy picture book!

Taste in picture books and stories for the under-fives is largely a personal affair. After all – you're the one who is going to do the telling. So a story which you yourself enjoy has a greater chance of success with your listener.

Poetry

Poetry for children is becoming a lively and entertaining ingredient in many publisher's lists. Look out for new poets and new anthologies of the old favourites as an addition to story time!

Music

Taste in music, as in stories, must remain a personal affair. If I had to choose a musical item for a *Play School* script going out next week I'd be choosing from many alternatives. And I could well end up with traditional nursery rhymes, shaking a bag of dried leaves in time to Mozart, banging a saucepan-lid with a wooden spoon, having a long, close look at the workings of a euphonium or hand-clapping the rhythm of the blues. All of these things find a place in *Play School.*

BBC Records from Play School

L.P. Cat. No.		Cassette Cat. No.
REC 212 Stereo	Sing A Song Of Play School	MRMC 031
REC 232 Stereo	The Tale Of A Donkey's Tail	MRMC 045
REC 242 Stereo	Bang On A Drum	MRMC 004
RBT 10	Play School	MRMC 005
REC 332	Play On (Songs From Play School)	ZCM 332
REC 425	Play School – Hello	ZCM 425

Acknowledgements

Acknowledgements are due to the following for permission to reproduce copyright material: The Abingdon Press for *I want to go on a Bear Hunt* from PLAY ACTIVITIES FOR THE RETARDED CHILD by Bernice Wells Carlson and David R. Ginglend, copyright © 1961 by Abingdon Press; Dobson Books Ltd. for *Today I saw a little worm* from SILLY VERSE FOR KIDS by Spike Milligan; B. Feldman and Co. Ltd. for *Oh we all dance the wibbly-wobbly walk*; Kensington Music Ltd. for *I'll take you riding in my car* by Woody Guthrie; George G. Harrap and Co. Ltd. for *Jump-jump Kangaroo Brown* by Linda Chesterman from MUSIC FOR THE NURSERY SCHOOL; Heathside Music Ltd. for *Those little ticks of time* by Matt McGinn; Oxford University Press and the authors for *'Who's that tickling my back?' said the wall* by Ian Serraillier, and *Let's all clap together* by William Clough.

Piles of golden oranges © Marcia Armitage 1971.

Here is a rocket that flew to the moon © Wilma Horsbrugh 1971.

How many puffs?, *Our fat black cat*, *Flutter your eye*, *Reach up and paint the ceiling*, *Have a blow, Jo!*, *Oh, I'm shaking like a jelly on a plate*, *If my shoes are on my hands*, *I'm a big beech tree*, *I'm the man*, *Both boots stuck in the mud*, *Miss Gloria Grand got ready for the dance*, *Mrs Slam-Bang stamped down the stairs* and *Johnny Brown had a frown* © Ruth Craft 1971. The remainder of the verses are from traditional sources.